Yum & Asian treats

KÖNEMANN

Glossary

The rich spices and herbs and distinctive ingredients of Asian cooking are familiar to most of us from restaurants and travels but can become daunting in our own kitchen. This can quickly be overcome with a little knowledge on how best to recognise and prepare them.

Bamboo Shoots
These are sold canned in water. Store the unused portion in water for up to one week, changing the water daily. These are available in Asian food stores and in the Asian section of large supermarkets.

Bean Curd (Tofu)
This is available fresh, dried and deep-fried, in firm and soft varieties. Made from soy beans, tofu is an excellent source of protein. Store fresh bean curd in water in the refrigerator, changing the water each day for up to 5 days. Fresh bean curd, even the firm variety, is quite soft and care needs to be taken when stirring or stir-frying so as not to break it up too much. Deep-fried bean curd has been fried to a golden brown colour and has a spongy texture. This needs to be used within 2–3 days of purchase and stored in an airtight container. It is available from Asian food stores, health food stores and supermarkets.

Bean Sprouts
The crisp sprouts of mung beans, bean sprouts deteriorate very rapidly and should be stored in water in the refrigerator for 1–2 days. Cooking time is very quick and bean sprouts will give a dish a crisp freshness. Traditional Asian cooks will always pick off the thin, scraggly tail.

Besan Flour
Made from ground chickpeas and used in Indian cuisine, besan flour has a distinctive flavour and texture. It is available from health food shops and some larger supermarkets.

Black Beans
These heavily salted, fermented soy beans must be well-rinsed before use. Available in cans or packets from Asian food stores, they keep indefinitely in an airtight container in the fridge.

❖ Glossary ❖

Black Fungus (Cloud Ear Fungus)

This member of the mushroom family is sold dried in packets. To use, it must be soaked in hot water until soft. The fungi will reconsitute to many times their dried size. They are included in dishes for their texture rather than flavour, which is quite mild. Available dried in packets from Asian food stores.

Cellophane / Dried Vermicelli Noodles

These are fine dried transparent noodles which are usually soaked in hot water until soft or may need to be boiled. They are available from Asian food stores and most supermarkets.

Chinese Sausage (Lup Chiang)

This spicy pork sausage needs to be steamed or baked before eating. Sold in the refrigerator section of Asian supermarkets, or in an airtight unrefrigerated packet in Asian food stores or butchers, it will keep up to 3 months in the refrigerator.

Coriander

This aromatic herb is used to flavour Asian food or as a garnish. The whole fresh plant is used—roots, stems and leaves. The seeds can be roasted whole but more often they are ground to a powder. Available dried in most spice sections, fresh coriander is also available from larger greengrocers.

Cumin

This aromatic spice is available both in seeds and ground. The flavour is more fully developed if the dish is dry-fried. Cumin is one of the important flavours in curry paste.

Fenugreek

These are aromatic seeds which are dry-fried and ground, then added to curry paste or used in Indian dishes. Use sparingly as the flavour can be bitter.

Fish Sauce

A pungent flavoured salty sauce, used widely in Thai and (in a darker variety) Vietnamese cooking. Available from Asian food stores and large supermarkets, fish sauce keeps indefinitely once opened. Store in the refrigerator.

3

❖ YUM CHA AND ASIAN TREATS ❖

Five-spice Powder
This aromatic ready-mixed ground spice mixture is used extensively in Chinese cooking. It should be used sparingly as it can overpower lesser flavours. Five-spice powder is available in the spices section of supermarkets and Asian food stores.

Flours
Asian rice flour is a finely ground short-grain rice flour. It has a fine light texture and gives a characteristic crunch to fried foods if used in a batter or as a coating.

Tapioca flour can be used as a substitute for cornflour. It is also used in doughs for many Asian treats.
Chinese wheat starch flour is an essential ingredient in translucent gow gee and dumpling dough. Flours are available from Asian or some health food stores.

Garlic Chives
The garlic chive is a wide and flat-leafed chive with a subtly flavoured stem and an attractive, edible flower. These are available from Asian and good fruit and vegetable specialists.

Hoi Sin Sauce
This is a thick red-brown sauce with a sweet-spicy flavour. It is made from soy beans and spices and is available from Asian food stores and supermarkets.

Mushrooms (Dried Chinese)
These are unique woody-flavoured mushrooms, which are sold dried. They are reconstituted in hot water until soft and spongy and should then be sliced or chopped and the hard stem discarded. Dried Chinese mushrooms are available in packets from Asian food stores and supermarkets.

Oyster Sauce
This is a rich smooth silky sauce and, although it is made from oysters and soy sauce it does not have a fishy flavour and is compatible with many foods. Keep refrigerated once the bottle is opened. Oyster sauce is available from Asian food stores and supermarkets.

Rice Paper Wrappers
Rice paper wrappers are made by forming a mixture of rice flour and water into very thin crepes and then drying these in the sun. The wrappers are very brittle in their dried form and they must be brushed with water to

❖ Glossary ❖

soften them up before use. Rice paper wrappers are available in Asian food stores.

Sesame Oil
This highly fragrant oil is made from sesame seeds. It is widely used in Chinese cooking. Sold in bottles, it is available from Asian food stores and most supermarkets. Sesame oil should be used sparingly.

Shaosing Wine (Chinese Wine)
This inexpensive Chinese cooking wine is available from Asian food stores. If you cannot find it, dry sherry can be substituted.

Soy Sauce
Soy sauce is made from fermented soy beans and is rich and salty in flavour. It is available in three varieties: light (standard) soy is most commonly used; dark soy is used for heavier meat and chicken dishes when a thicker darker colour is needed and mushroom soy has mushrooms added during the last stages of processing. All are available in bottles from Asian food stores and good supermarkets. Soy sauce keeps indefinitely.

Preserved Turnip
This is a salted and preserved turnip which adds a delicious flavour, but must be used sparingly. It is available in packets from Asian food stores. Once the packet has been opened it must be kept refrigerated.

Wasabi
This highly pungent green horseradish paste is used in Japanese cooking. It is available in a paste, dried or powdered from Asian specialty stores and is used sparingly.

Water Chestnuts
These sweet vegetables are very crunchy and crisp in texture. They are available canned, from Asian food stores and supermarkets. They should be stored in water, which needs to be changed daily, and they will keep for 3-4 days. They are occasionally available from Asian fruit and vegetable shops.

Won Ton Wrappers / Spring Roll Wrappers
These thin dough portions are sold in squares or rounds, both fresh and frozen. They are sold in Asian food stores or some large supermarkets and can be kept in the freezer until needed. When filling, work with one at a time and keep the others covered with a damp tea towel to prevent drying out.

Yum Cha

Centuries ago the chefs of Imperial China created succulent bite-sized snacks to be enjoyed as a selection of different tastes and textures. These have survived the years and are now taken with tea and known as Yum Cha.

Vietnamese Lettuce-wrapped Spring Rolls

Preparation time:
  50 minutes
Total cooking time:
  20 minutes
Makes 20

50 g cellophane noodles
2 tablespoons dried black fungus
2 cups hot water
20–25 rice paper wrappers
250 g raw prawn meat
150 g pork mince
4 spring onions, chopped
1/2 cup bean sprouts, roughly chopped
1 teaspoon sugar
salt and pepper, to taste
1 egg, beaten
oil, for deep frying

To serve
20 lettuce leaves
1 cup bean sprouts
1 cup mint leaves

Dipping Sauce
2 tablespoons fish sauce
2 tablespoons cold water
1 teaspoon soft brown sugar
1 teaspoon chopped chilli
2 tablespoons chopped coriander

1. Soak the noodles and fungus, separately, in hot water for 10 minutes, or until soft. Drain and chop the fungus roughly and then set aside.
2. Using a pastry brush, brush each rice paper wrapper liberally with water. Allow to stand for 2 minutes or until they become soft and pliable; stack on a plate. Finely chop the prawn meat and combine with the pork mince, spring onions, bean sprouts, sugar, salt and pepper, noodles and fungus in a bowl. Stir well. Place 1 tablespoon of filling along the base of the wrapper. Fold in sides and roll up tightly. Brush the seam with egg and place on a baking tray. Repeat with the remaining wrappers and filling.
3. Press the rolls with paper towels to remove any excess water. Heat 4–5 cm oil in a pan; add the spring rolls in batches and cook for 2–3 minutes or until dark golden brown. Drain on paper towels.
4. Place a spring roll in each lettuce leaf, top with 1 tablespoon bean sprouts and 2 mint leaves. Roll up to form a neat parcel. Serve with dipping sauce.
5. To make dipping sauce: Combine the sauce, water, sugar, chilli and coriander in a bowl and stir well.

Note: Rice paper wrappers are available from Asian food stores, and are dry and brittle until they are moistened with water. Keep them stacked up so that they stay moist and work with one at a time. Have a few extra on hand as they can break easily.

Vietnamese Lettuce-wrapped Spring Rolls

❖ YUM CHA AND ASIAN TREATS ❖

Honeyed Chicken Pieces

Preparation time:
  15 minutes +
  12 hours marinating
Total cooking time:
  15 minutes
Makes about 15

2 teaspoons honey
2 teaspoons hot water
2 teaspoons
  lemon juice
2 cloves garlic, crushed
2 teaspoons grated
  ginger
2 chicken breast fillets
salt and pepper, to taste
oil, for deep frying

Batter
1 tablespoon plain flour
2 teaspoons oil
2 tablespoons water
2 teaspoons honey
1 tablespoon soy sauce
1 tablespoon sherry
1 egg white

1. Combine the honey, water, lemon juice, garlic and ginger in a bowl. Slice the chicken into thin strips; transfer to a non-metal dish and brush with the honey mixture. Cover the dish and refrigerate for 12 hours. Season the chicken with salt and pepper and drain well.
2. To make batter: Combine the flour, oil, water, honey, soy sauce and sherry in a bowl; mix until smooth. Whisk the egg white until light and fluffy. Quickly fold into the flour mixture.
3. Dip the chicken pieces into the batter, draining excess. Heat 3–4 cm oil in a pan; add the chicken pieces, a few at a time, and cook for 2 minutes or until deep golden brown. Remove from the oil; drain on paper towels. Serve hot.

Chilli Calamari

Preparation time:
  10 minutes +
  30 minutes standing
Total cooking time:
  10 minutes
Serves 4–6

3 calamari hoods, sliced
1 egg
2 tablespoons sweet
  chilli sauce
1 tablespoon soy sauce
1 teaspoon chopped
  fresh coriander leaves
1/2 teaspoon
  chopped chilli
oil, for shallow frying

1. Combine the calamari, egg, sauces, coriander and chilli. Leave for at least 30 minutes. Drain well.
2. Heat 1–2 cm oil in a pan; add the calamari in batches and cook for 1–2 minutes or until golden. Good with sweet chilli sauce.

Prawn and Coriander Toast

Preparation time:
  15 minutes
Total cooking time:
  15 minutes
Makes 32

500 g raw prawns,
  shelled and deveined
8 spring onions, chopped
1 stalk lemon grass,
  chopped
1 clove garlic, crushed
1 egg white
1 tablespoon oil
1 tablespoon chopped
  fresh coriander leaves
1 tablespoon fish sauce
2 teaspoons chilli sauce
1 teaspoon lemon juice
8 slices stale bread,
  crusts removed
oil, for shallow frying

1. Combine the prawns, spring onions, lemon grass, garlic, egg white, oil, coriander, sauces and lemon juice in a food processor. Process until finely chopped.
2. Spread the prawn mixture generously over the bread. Cut each slice into 4 triangles.
3. Heat 1–2 cm oil in a pan; add the bread and cook, prawn side down,

❖ YUM CHA AND ASIAN TREATS ❖

Prawn and Coriander Toast (top); Honeyed Chicken Pieces (left) and Chilli Calamari

---

for 2–3 minutes. Turn over and cook the other side for 1 minute or until golden and crisp. Drain well on paper towels.

Note: Royal red prawns can be bought already shelled.

❖ YUM CHA AND ASIAN TREATS ❖

Scallop and Ginger Pockets

Preparation time:
40 minutes
Total cooking time:
15 minutes
Makes 25

1 tablespoon oil
5 cm ginger, peeled, sliced and shredded
4 spring onions, finely chopped
25 scallops, red coral removed (350 g)
1 tablespoon Shaosing (Chinese) wine or sherry
2 teaspoons sesame oil
1 teaspoon cornflour
salt and pepper, to taste
25 won ton or egg noodle wrappers
1 egg, beaten
oil, for shallow frying
1/2 bunch garlic chives

1. Heat the oil in a pan; add the ginger and spring onions and cook over medium heat for 2 minutes, stirring occasionally. Increase heat and when pan is very hot, add scallops and stir-fry, tossing quickly, for 30 seconds. Remove pan from heat.
2. Combine the wine, sesame oil, cornflour, salt and pepper in a bowl and blend to a smooth paste. Pour over the scallops, return pan to heat and toss over high heat for 30 seconds or until liquid has thickened. Cool completely.
3. Working with one wrapper at a time (keeping the rest covered), lightly brush edge of wrapper with beaten egg. Place a scallop in the centre, bring up sides and pinch together to form a pouch, leaving a frill at the top. Place on a baking tray and repeat with remaining wrappers and filling.
4. Heat 1–2 cm oil in a pan; add the scallop pouches (in batches, if necessary) and cook for 4–5 minutes or until golden brown. Drain on paper towels. Tie a chive around each and serve immediately.

Note: Use Chinese scallops, if possible. These are available from seafood markets or Chinese seafood shops and are bigger and whiter than other scallops with no red coral. If using other scallops, remove the red coral and double the quantity above.

Scallop and Ginger Pockets (left) and Steamed Rice Balls

Steamed Rice Balls

Preparation time:
25 minutes + 30 minutes standing
Total cooking time:
30 minutes
Makes about 24

1 cup rice
500 g pork mince
4 spring onions, chopped
1 tablespoon chopped water chestnuts
1 tablespoon oyster sauce
2 teaspoons sweet chilli sauce
3 cloves garlic, crushed
1 tablespoon grated fresh ginger
1 tablespoon salt

1. Soak the rice in cold water for 30 minutes. Drain well.
2. Combine the mince, spring onions, water chestnuts, sauces, garlic, ginger and salt in a bowl and roll into walnut-sized balls. Coat each ball in rice.
3. Put the rice balls, well spaced, in a single layer in steamer. (Cook in batches, if necessary.) Cover and place over a pan of simmering water for 25–30 minutes or until rice is tender and balls are cooked through. Serve with dipping sauce.

Thai Corn Pancakes

Preparation time:
25 minutes
Total cooking time:
20 minutes
Makes about 15

2 cups frozen
  corn kernels
3 spring onions,
  finely sliced
4 cm piece ginger,
  finely grated
2 cloves garlic, crushed
1/2 cup chopped
  coriander leaves
1/4 cup cornflour
2 eggs, beaten
2 teaspoons fish sauce
1 teaspoon soft
  brown sugar
oil, for shallow frying

1. Combine the corn, spring onion, ginger, garlic and coriander in a large bowl. Blend the cornflour, egg, fish sauce and sugar in a separate bowl; stir into corn mixture and beat with a wooden spoon.
2. Heat 1–2 cm oil in a large pan; add a tablespoon of mixture and cook over medium heat for 2 minutes or until crisp on base. Turn over gently and cook other side for 1 minute. Repeat with remaining mixture. Drain on paper towels and serve immediately.

Spicy Fish Skewers

Preparation time:
10 minutes +
1 hour refrigeration
Total cooking time:
10 minutes
Makes about 12

1 green chilli, seeded
1 clove garlic, crushed
2 spring onions,
  chopped
1 teaspoon grated
  ginger
1/2 teaspoon ground
  coriander
40 g macadamia nuts,
  chopped
1 stem lemon grass,
  finely chopped
1 tablespoon oil
250 g white fish fillets
1 tablespoon soy sauce
salt and black pepper,
  to taste

1. Combine the chilli, garlic, spring onion, ginger, coriander, macadamia nuts and lemon grass in a food processor. Process until mixture becomes a smooth paste.
2. Heat the oil in a pan and cook paste over medium heat for 4 minutes or until golden brown. Allow to cool.
3. Process the fish in a food processor until very finely minced. Add the cooked paste, soy sauce, salt and pepper and process to blend together. Refrigerate until chilled through (about 1 hour).
4. Mould heaped tablespoons of the mixture around wooden skewers. Cook under a preheated hot grill for 3 minutes on each side or until golden brown. Serve hot with satay sauce.

Deep-Fried Carrot Balls

Preparation time:
25 minutes
Total cooking time:
15 minutes
Makes about 20

350 g carrot, peeled
  and sliced
2 cm piece fresh ginger,
  peeled and grated
2 spring onions, finely
  chopped
2 teaspoons sesame oil
1 egg, beaten
salt and pepper, to taste
3/4 cup plain flour
1/3 cup sesame seeds
oil, for deep frying

1. Cook the carrot in boiling salted water for 15 minutes until just tender. Drain and mash well. Place the ginger in a garlic crusher and squeeze the juice into the mashed carrot. Add the spring onions,

❖ YUM CHA AND ASIAN TREATS ❖

Clockwise from left: Carrot Balls; Spicy Fish Skewers; Thai Corn Pancakes

sesame oil and egg and season to taste.
2. Shape the carrot mixture into small, walnut-sized balls. Roll the balls in the combined flour and sesame seeds, shaking off the excess.
3. Heat 3–4 cm oil in a pan; add the carrot balls and cook in batches for 2–3 minutes or until golden.

Remove the balls from the pan, drain on paper towels, then return to the oil and cook for another 30 seconds. Drain on paper towels and serve immediately.

13

❖ YUM CHA AND ASIAN TREATS ❖

Spring Rolls

Traditionally these crisply fried rolls were filled with fresh bamboo shoots and served as a tasty treat at the spring festival. Today they have come to epitomise all we enjoy about the taste of China.

Traditional Spring Rolls
Heat 1 tablespoon oil in a wok or pan, add 2 cloves chopped garlic, 3 cm grated ginger and cook for 30 seconds. Add 100 g pork mince, 100 g chicken mince and 50 g minced raw prawn meat to the pan. Stir-fry for 3 minutes to brown the mince. Transfer the mixture to a bowl. Wipe the pan clean and add 1 tablespoon oil, 2 sticks finely sliced celery, 1 small finely chopped carrot, 1/2 cup chopped water chestnuts, 4 chopped spring onions and 1 cup finely shredded cabbage. Stir over medium heat for 2 minutes. Blend 1/2 cup chicken stock, 1 tablespoon cornflour, 2 tablespoons oyster sauce, 1 tablespoon soy sauce and 1/2 teaspoon each of salt and white pepper and mix until smooth. Stir into the vegetables and stir until the sauce has thickened. Add 2 teaspoons sesame oil to the cooked meat mixture. Stir well and allow to cool.

Blend 1/4 cup extra cornflour with 1/3 cup water and mix until smooth. Take 2 small square spring roll wrappers and place one on the bench with a corner facing you. Brush all the edges with a little cornflour paste and lay the second sheet on top. Brush the edges of the second sheet with cornflour paste. Spread about 1 1/2 tablespoons of the filling across the bottom corner of the wrapper. Fold the bottom corner up over the filling, fold in the sides and roll up firmly. Repeat with the remaining wrappers and filling. Heat 3 cups oil in a deep pan and fry the rolls, in batches, for 2–3 minutes or until a deep golden brown. Drain on paper towels and serve with a sweet chilli sauce and soy sauce. Makes 18.

From left: Traditional; Vegetarian; Thai; Prawn and Crab Spring Rolls

❖ Spring Rolls ❖

Vegetarian Filling
Heat 1 tablespoon oil in a wok or pan and add 2 cloves chopped garlic, 4 chopped spring onions, 4 cm sliced and finely shredded ginger. Stir over medium heat for 2 minutes. Add 2 sticks finely sliced celery, 2 cups grated carrot, 2 cups finely shredded cabbage, 1/2 cup finely sliced deep-fried bean curd, 1 cup bean shoots and 2 tablespoons chopped water chestnuts. Cover the pan and steam the mixture for 2 minutes. Blend 3 teaspoons cornflour with 1 tablespoon water, 2 teaspoons sesame oil, 2 teaspoons soy sauce and 1/2 teaspoon salt and white pepper and mix until smooth. Stir into the vegetable mixture and stir for 2 minutes or until the sauce has thickened. Leave it to cool completely. Make the rolls as above.

Thai Filling
Soak 30 g dried vermicelli noodles in hot water until soft then drain well. Heat 1 tablespoon oil in a wok or pan and add 3 cloves chopped garlic, 3 cm grated galangal or ginger, 3 finely chopped coriander roots and 3 chopped spring onions. Stir-fry for 2 minutes. Add 200 g pork mince and 2 sticks finely sliced celery to the pan. Stir-fry for 3 minutes to brown the pork, breaking up any lumps. Add 1 cup grated carrot, 1/2 cup chopped coriander, 1/4 cup finely chopped cucumber, 1 tablespoon sweet chilli sauce, 2 teaspoons fish sauce and 1 teaspoon brown sugar and mix well. Cool completely. Make up the rolls as above.

Prawn and Crab Filling
Heat 1 tablespoon oil in a wok, stir-fry 2 chopped cloves of garlic, 4 cm grated fresh ginger and 4 chopped spring onions for 1 minute. Add 350 g chopped raw prawn meat and stir-fry for 3 mintues. Add 1 cup roughly chopped bean sprouts, 1/4 cup chopped water chestnuts and 2 tablespoons roughly chopped fresh peppercorns. Stir in 225 g canned drained crab meat and 2 tablespoons chopped coriander leaves. Mix 1 tablespoon cornflour with 1 tablespoon water, 1 tablespoon fish sauce, 1 teaspoon brown sugar and 1/4 teaspoon salt until smooth. Stir into the prawn mixture and cook until thickened. Cool, then make up the rolls as above.

❖ YUM CHA AND ASIAN TREATS ❖

1 Finely shred the won ton wrappers with a sharp knife.

2 Cut a shallow incision along the underside of each prawn.

Stuffed Prawns in Crispy Won Ton

Preparation time:
  40 minutes
Total cooking time:
  10 minutes
Makes 12

15 won ton wrappers
12 large raw prawns
200 g raw prawn meat
4 spring onions, very
  finely chopped
50 g pork fat, finely
  chopped
1 egg white
1/2 cup cornflour
salt and pepper, to taste
1 egg, lightly beaten
oil, for deep frying

1. Using a very sharp paring knife, thinly shred the won ton wrappers. Peel the prawns, leaving the tails intact. Discard the heads. Using the tip of a small sharp knife, pull out the dark vein. Cut a shallow incision along the inside of the prawn.
2. Combine the prawn meat, spring onions and pork fat on a chopping board. Using a large sharp knife, chop the mixture until very smooth. (Alternatively, roughly chop in a food processor.) Place the mixture in a bowl and add the egg white, 3 teaspoons of the cornflour, salt and pepper and mix together very well with your fingertips.
3. Using a knife, spread about 1 tablespoon of the prawn mixture along each prawn, pressing as much mixture as possible into the pocket. With wet hands, press any remaining mixture around the prawn. Coat each prawn in the remaining cornflour, lightly dip in egg, then loosely sprinkle with won ton shreds, pressing very firmly.
4. Heat 3–4 cm oil in a wok or pan, add the prawns in batches and cook for 4 minutes or until golden brown. Drain on paper towels and serve immediately.

Note: The prawns can be cleaned and filled with stuffing up to a day in advance. Store in the refrigerator. Coat the prawns with shredded won ton just before frying.
Pork fat is available in the refrigerator section of Asian supermarkets.

Stuffed Prawns in Crispy Won Ton

3 Spread the stuffing along the incision in the prawn, pressing firmly.

4 Carefully coat the stuffed prawns in cornflour before dipping in egg.

Samosas

Preparation time:
  30 minutes
Total cooking time:
  10–15 minutes
Makes about 24

2 potatoes, peeled
1/2 cup frozen peas
1/4 cup currants
2 tablespoons chopped
  fresh coriander
2 tablespoons
  lemon juice
1 tablespoon soy sauce
1 teaspoon ground
  cumin
1 teaspoon ground
  chilli powder
1/2 teaspoon chopped
  fresh chilli
1/4 teaspoon ground
  cinnamon
4 sheets ready-rolled
  frozen puff pastry,
  thawed
oil, for shallow frying

Mint Sauce
1/2 cup plain yoghurt
1/2 cup buttermilk
1/4 cup finely chopped
  fresh mint
1/2 teaspoon ground
  cumin

1. Cook the potatoes until tender and chop finely. Mix together the potatoes, peas, currants, coriander, lemon juice, soy sauce, cumin, chilli powder, chilli and cinnamon.

2. Cut the pastry into rounds using a 10 cm cutter. Place teaspoonful of the mixture on one side of each round. Fold the pastry over the filling to make a semi-circle. Press the edges together firmly with a fork.

3. Heat 1–2 cm oil in pan; add the pastries and cook for 2–3 minutes each side or until golden brown and puffed. Drain on paper towels. Serve with Mint Sauce.

4. **To make Mint Sauce:** Combine the yoghurt, buttermilk, mint and cumin and stir until smooth.

Deep-fried Oysters

Preparation time:
  35 minutes +
  30 minutes standing
Total cooking time:
  10–15 minutes
Makes 24

Batter
1/2 cup plain flour
1/3 cup cornflour
1/3 cup rice flour
1 tablespoon baking
  powder
1 teaspoon salt
1 1/2 cups cold water
2 tablespoons oil

24 large plump oysters
1 teaspoon salt
1 tablespoon cornflour
2 teaspoons oil
3 cm ginger, peeled and
  finely grated
3 spring onions, finely
  chopped
2 teaspoons Chinese
  (Shaosing) wine
1/4 teaspoon white
  pepper
oil, for deep frying

Dipping Sauce
2 tablespoons soy sauce
2 teaspoons
  Worcestershire sauce
1/2 teaspoon sesame oil

1. **To make batter:** Sift flours, baking powder and salt into a large bowl; make a well in the centre and gradually stir in enough water and oil, alternately, to make a thick batter. Set aside for 30 minutes to thicken.

2. Place the oysters in a bowl with the salt and cornflour; mix well. Rinse very well under cold running water. Plunge the oysters into boiling water for 30 seconds then drain.

3. Heat the oil in a pan; add the ginger and spring onions and cook for 1 minute over medium heat. Add the wine and pepper. Transfer to a bowl. Add the oysters and stir to combine. Stir the batter well. Heat 4–5 cm oil in a large pan. Using two

❖ YUM CHA AND ASIAN TREATS ❖

Samosas with Mint Sauce (top) and Deep-fried Oysters

spoons, dip the oysters into the batter, draining the excess. Fry the oysters in batches for 2–3 minutes or until all are golden and puffed. Drain well on paper towels and serve immediately with Dipping Sauce.

4. To make Dipping Sauce: Combine the soy and Worcestershire sauces and oil and stir.

Note: Salting the oysters and mixing them with cornflour draws out any grit and impurities which are then washed away under the cold water.

Vegetable Pakoras

Preparation time:
15 minutes
Total cooking time:
20 minutes
Serves 4

1 cup besan flour (chickpea flour)
1/2 teaspoon ground coriander
1/2 teaspoon ground turmeric
1/2 teaspoon chilli powder
1/2 teaspoon garam masala
1 teaspoon salt
1–2 cloves garlic
3/4 cup water
1/2 cauliflower, cut into florets
2 onions, peeled and sliced into rings
oil, for deep frying

1. Sift the flour into a bowl; add the coriander, turmeric, chilli powder, garam masala, salt and garlic.
2. Make a well in the centre and gradually add the water to form a thick, smooth batter.
3. Coat the vegetables in batter. Heat 3–4 cm oil in a deep pan and cook the cauliflower and onions in batches for 4–5 minutes or until golden. Drain on paper towels. Serve with mint sauce, if desired.

Note: Small pickling onions are good for making pakoras. You can also use thick slices of eggplant or potato, or broccoli florets.

Paper-wrapped Prawns

Preparation time:
35 minutes
Total cooking time:
5–10 minutes
Makes 12 parcels

15–20 rice paper wrappers
350 g raw prawn meat
4 cm piece fresh ginger, grated
2 cloves garlic, crushed
3 spring onions, finely chopped
1 tablespoon rice flour
1 egg white, beaten
2 teaspoons sesame oil
salt and pepper, to taste
2 tablespoons cornflour
6 teaspoons water
oil, for deep frying
2 tablespoons sesame seeds, toasted

1. Place 4 rice paper wrappers on a work surface. Brush generously with water to moisten; allow to stand for 2 minutes or until soft and pliable. Gently transfer to a plate (they may be stacked on top of each other at this stage). Cover with plastic wrap and repeat with remaining wrappers.
2. Finely chop the prawn meat; combine with the ginger, garlic, spring onions, rice flour, egg white, sesame oil and salt and pepper. Mix very well with your fingertips. Blend the cornflour and water. Working with one wrapper at a time, spread 1 tablespoon of prawn mixture across the wrapper just below the centre. Fold up the bottom section of the wrapper to encase the filling. Roll wrapper over once, lightly pushing down to flatten out filling. Fold in sides and brush edges with cornflour mixture, then wrap to form a parcel. Put on double thickness paper towels and repeat with remaining wrappers and filling.
3. Heat 2–3 cm oil in a deep pan; add several parcels and cook for 4–5 minutes or until golden brown. Drain on paper towels and repeat with remainder. Sprinkle with sesame seeds. Serve with plum sauce, if desired.

Paper-wrapped Prawns (top) and Vegetable Pakoras

❖ Yum Cha and Asian Treats ❖

❖ Yum Cha and Asian Treats ❖

Dumplings

These miniature bite-sized pouches of chopped meat, seafood or vegetables, encased in near translucent won ton wrappers, can be served steamed or crisply fried. All make about 30 dumplings.

Pork Dumplings
Put 250 g pork mince, 125 g chopped raw prawn meat, 1/4 cup chopped bamboo shoots, 3 finely chopped spring onions, 3 chopped mushrooms, 1 stick of chopped celery, 1/2 a chopped capsicum, 1 tablespoon dry sherry, 1 tablespoon soy sauce, 1 teaspoon sesame oil and 1/2 teaspoon chopped chilli in a bowl. Mix well. Place about 1 teaspoon of the filling in the centre of each won ton wrapper. Brush the edges with a little water. Fold over to make a triangle with the points slightly overlapping. Press together firmly. Bring two ends together to make a round dumpling. Press the ends together firmly. (Alternatively, gather the wrapper around filling to form a pouch, slightly open at the top.) Deep-fry in hot oil for 4–5 minutes or steam in a bamboo or metal steamer for 25–30 minutes. Serve with dipping sauce.

Below, left to right: Pork; Prawn; Pork and Tofu; Crabmeat and Chicken Dumplings

❖ DUMPLINGS ❖

FILLING VARIETIES

Prawn Dumplings
Process 500 g raw prawn meat, 125 g pork mince, 4 chopped spring onions, 60 g mushrooms, $1/4$ cup chopped water chestnuts, 1 tablespoon dry sherry, 1 tablespoon soy sauce, 1 egg white and 1 teaspoon sesame oil in a food processor until smooth. Make the dumplings as above.

Pork and Tofu Dumplings
Cook 250 g pork mince in a little oil until browned. Add 2 cups finely shredded Chinese cabbage, 1 cup bean sprouts, 4 finely chopped spring onions and 1 grated carrot. Stir over heat until cabbage wilts. Add 60 g chopped tofu, 2 cloves crushed garlic, 2 teaspoons grated fresh ginger, 2 tablespoons dry sherry, 1 tablespoon soy sauce and 1 teaspoon sesame oil. Mix well, cool, then make dumplings as above.

Crabmeat Dumplings
Combine 200 g drained and flaked crabmeat, 125 g raw prawn meat, 4 finely chopped spring onions, 3 soaked and chopped dried mushrooms, $1/4$ cup finely chopped bean sprouts, 1 tablespoon teriyaki sauce, 2 cloves crushed garlic and 2 teaspoons grated fresh ginger in a bowl. Make the dumplings as above.

Chicken Dumplings
Combine 375 g chicken mince, 90 g finely chopped ham, 4 finely chopped spring onions, 1 stick finely chopped celery, $1/4$ cup chopped bamboo shoots, 1 tablespoon soy sauce, 1 clove crushed garlic and 1 teaspoon grated fresh ginger in a bowl. Make the dumplings as above.

Thai Fish Cakes

Preparation time:
  15 minutes
Total cooking time:
  15 minutes
Makes about 24

250 g boneless fish
  fillets, chopped
4 spring onions, chopped
2 cloves garlic, crushed
2 tablespoons chopped
  fresh coriander
1 egg
1 tablespoon Thai
  fish sauce
2 teaspoons chilli sauce
1 teaspoon soy sauce
1/2 teaspoon finely
  grated lime rind
1 tablespoon lime juice
1/2 teaspoon chopped
  chilli
1/2 cup rice flour
oil, for shallow frying

1. Process the fish, spring onions, garlic, coriander, egg, sauces, lime rind and juice, chilli and rice flour in a food processor for 60 seconds or until finely chopped and mixed.
2. With oiled hands, shape the mixture into small patties. Heat 1–2 cm oil in a pan and cook the patties over medium heat for 2–3 minutes each side or until golden. Drain well and serve with sweet chilli sauce, if desired.

Note: Dust the patties lightly in cornflour before frying to give a crisp finish.

Chilli and Black Bean Pork Ribs

Preparation time:
  20 minutes +
  1 hour standing
Total cooking time:
  30 minutes
Serves 4–6

1 tablespoon black
  beans
1 teaspoon oil
1 tablespoon grated
  ginger
1–2 cloves garlic,
  crushed
1–2 teaspoons chopped
  fresh chillies
2 tablespoons Chinese
  wine or sherry
2 teaspoons soy sauce
2 teaspoons caster sugar
500 g pork ribs, cut
  into bite-sized pieces

1. Soak the black beans in 2 tablespoons water for 10 minutes; rinse.
2. Heat the oil in a frying pan, add the ginger, garlic and chilli and stir-fry over medium heat for 1 minute. Add the black beans, wine, soy sauce and sugar; cook for another minute, stirring constantly. Pour sauce over the ribs, tossing well to coat. Cover and refrigerate for 1 hour.
3. Line the base of a bamboo or metal steamer with baking paper. Arrange the ribs, well spaced, on the paper. (Cook in batches, if necessary.) Place the steamer over a pan of simmering water, cover and cook the pork for about 30 minutes or until firm to touch and cooked through. Serve with chilli sauce, if desired.

Prawn Cutlets

Preparation time:
  20 minutes +
  30 minutes standing
Total cooking time:
  10–15 minutes
Serves 4–6

1 kg raw king prawns
1/3 cup plain flour
1/4 teaspoon five-
  spice powder
1 egg, lightly beaten
2 tablespoons milk
1 cup breadcrumbs
oil, for deep frying

1. Shell and devein the prawns, leaving the tails intact. Make a deep cut along the back of each prawn, taking care not to cut right through. Flatten the prawns with the palm of your hand.

YUM CHA AND ASIAN TREATS

From top: Chilli and Black Bean Pork Ribs, Thai Fish Cakes and Prawn Cutlets

2. Combine the flour and five-spice powder; dust the prawns in the mixture, shaking off excess. Dip the prawns in the combined egg and milk then coat in breadcrumbs. Arrange in a single layer on a tray or plate and chill for at least 30 minutes.
3. Heat 4–5 cm oil in a pan; add the prawn cutlets and cook for 2–3 minutes each side or until golden and crisp. Drain well on paper towels. Serve with satay, sweet and sour, soy or chilli sauces, if desired.

❖ YUM CHA AND ASIAN TREATS ❖

Crisp-fried Duck with Lemon Sauce

Preparation time:
40 minutes
Total cooking time:
60 minutes
Serves 10

1.3 kg duck
2 tablespoons soy sauce
1 tablespoon sesame oil
3 cm piece of ginger
3 spring onions,
  roughly chopped
oil, for deep frying

Lemon Sauce
1/4 cup lemon juice
1/4 cup water
1 teaspoon cornflour
2 teaspoons
  caster sugar
1 teaspoon vinegar
1/4 teaspoon salt
2–3 drops yellow
  food colouring

Batter
1 egg, lightly beaten
1 1/2 tablespoons
  cornflour
1 tablespoon water
2 teaspoons soy sauce
1/2 teaspoon
  bicarbonate of soda
salt and pepper, to taste

1. Cut the duck into four sections; trim the excess skin from the neck and trim fat from inside legs. Combine the soy sauce and sesame oil, brush lightly over the duck. Place the duck in a bamboo steamer. Bring a large pan of water to the boil, reduce the heat to a simmer; add the ginger piece and spring onion. Place the steamer over water; cover and cook for 30 minutes or until the duck is just cooked. Allow to cool. (Reserve the water for stock, if you like. See Note.)
2. **To make Lemon Sauce:** Combine the lemon juice, water, cornflour, sugar, vinegar and salt in a pan and stir well until smooth. Cook over medium heat, stirring constantly, until the sauce boils and thickens. Boil for another minute; stir in the food colouring and transfer to a small serving bowl. Cover the surface of the sauce with plastic wrap and set aside until needed.
3. Using a Chinese cleaver or large sharp knife, remove the duck wings and drumsticks. Chop the body of the duck into 2 cm long pieces, complete with bone. Remove the meat from the drumsticks and chop into small, neat pieces; discard the wings.
4. Combine the egg, cornflour, water, soy sauce, soda, salt and pepper in a bowl and beat with a wooden spoon until the batter is smooth. Heat 4–5 cm oil in a pan. Dip the duck pieces in batter, drain the excess and add to the pan. Cook over high heat for 2 minutes or until crisp and brown all over. (Cook the duck in batches, if necessary: do not overcrowd the pan or it will stew rather than fry.) Drain on paper towels and serve immediately with Lemon Sauce. Garnish with chargrilled banana or thin lemon slices and shredded spring onion.

Note: Adding ginger and spring onion to the simmering water will produce a pleasant aroma while steaming the duck and give you a light duck stock to use in soups. If you prefer to remove the wings and not eat them, cut them off before cooking and place them in the water with the ginger and spring onion to give the stock extra flavour. The duck can be steamed a day in advance of serving if necessary.

Crisp-fried Duck with Lemon Sauce

❖ YUM CHA AND ASIAN TREATS ❖

1 Carefully turn the pancake with a spatula and cook the other side.

2 Add the bean sprouts and cucumber to the filling mixture.

Prawn Pancake Rolls

Preparation time:
  45 minutes
Total cooking time:
  35 minutes
Makes 12

1 1/2 cups plain flour
2 1/2 cups water
2 eggs, beaten
salt and pepper, to taste
3 tablespoons oil

Filling
1 tablespoon oil
3 cm piece grated fresh ginger
1 large carrot, peeled and grated
1 stick celery, finely chopped
150 g raw prawn meat, finely chopped
1 cup bean sprouts
1/4 cup finely chopped cucumber
2 tablespoons sherry
1 tablespoon soy sauce
2 teaspoons sesame oil
2 teaspoons cornflour
2 eggs, beaten
1/4 cup water
2 teaspoons cornflour
2 tablespoons oil, extra

1. Sift the flour into a bowl; make a well in the centre. Add the water and eggs and mix to a smooth batter. Season with salt and pepper. Heat 1/2 teaspoon oil in a small non-stick frying pan; add 2 tablespoons batter and swirl until it begins to set. Cook for 30 seconds, turn and cook the other side for 10 seconds. Turn out and repeat with remaining batter.
2. To make filling: Heat the oil in a pan; add the ginger, carrot and celery and cook, over high heat, for 2 minutes. Add the prawn meat; cook for 1 minute or until the meat begins to turn pink. Add the bean sprouts and cucumber; remove from the heat. Blend the sherry, soy, oil and cornflour to a smooth paste. Add to the prawn mixture, return to the heat and bring to the boil. Remove from heat and allow to cool.
3. Spoon about a tablespoon of mixture across the centre of each pancake. Fold the pancakes over the filling, bringing in the edges and rolling over into neat flat parcels.
4. Combine the egg, water and cornflour in a shallow dish and use to coat the rolls. Heat the oil in a frying pan; add the pancakes and cook for 2 minutes each side until golden. Serve immediately.

Prawn Pancake Rolls

3 Spoon the mixture along the centre of each pancake and fold over to enclose.

4 Cook the pancakes for 2 minutes on each side until golden brown.

❖ YUM CHA AND ASIAN TREATS ❖

Thai Puffs

Preparation time:
  15 minutes
Total cooking time:
  20 minutes
Makes 36

2 tablespoons oil
4 spring onions, chopped
1 onion, chopped
1 clove garlic, crushed
250 g pork or
  chicken mince
1 tablespoon Thai
  flavour base (see
  Note)
1 cup mashed potato
4 sheets ready-rolled
  frozen puff pastry,
  thawed
oil, for frying

1. Heat the oil in a frying pan. Add the spring onions, onion and garlic and cook for 2–3 minutes or until the onion is tender. Add the mince and brown well for 4–5 minutes, breaking up with a spoon as it cooks. Stir in the flavour base and mashed potato and stir for 1 minute. Remove from heat and cool.
2. Cut each sheet of pastry into 9 even squares. Place teaspoonsful of the mixture in the centre of each piece of pastry. Fold the pastry over to form a triangle. Seal well by pressing the edges with a fork.
3. Heat 2–3 cm oil in a large frying pan; add the pastries, in batches, and fry for 2 minutes each side until golden and puffy. Drain well on paper towels. Good with sweet chilli sauce.

Note: If Thai flavour base is unavailable, add chopped lemon grass, coriander, chilli and a dash of fish sauce to the filling instead.

Crispy Vegetable Fritters

Preparation time:
  20 minutes
Total cooking time:
  10–15 minutes
Makes about 24

1/2 cup self-raising flour
1/4 cup besan flour
1 tablespoon chopped
  fresh coriander
1 teaspoon ground
  chilli powder
1/2 teaspoon garam
  masala
1/4 teaspoon ground
  cumin
1/4 teaspoon curry
  powder
1 clove garlic, crushed
1/2 cup water
130 g can corn kernels,
  drained
1 potato, peeled and
  finely chopped
1 zucchini, finely
  chopped
1 carrot, finely chopped
1/2 cup finely chopped
  cauliflower
oil, for shallow frying

1. Sift the flours into a large bowl. Add the coriander, chilli, garam masala, cumin, curry powder and garlic. Make a well in the centre of the flour mixture. Gradually add the water, beating well to form a smooth batter.
2. Add the corn, potato, zucchini, carrot and cauliflower to the batter. Mix well and season to taste.
3. Heat 1–2 cm oil in a frying pan. Add tablespoons of the mixture to the oil and cook in batches for 2–3 minutes each side or until golden and puffed. Drain well on paper towels. Serve with chilli sauce, if desired.

Note: Besan flour (chickpea flour) is available in health food stores. If you cannot find it use all self-raising flour.

Thai Puffs (top) and Crispy Vegetable Fritters

Beef Balls with Spicy Sausage

Preparation time:
35 minutes
Total cooking time:
30 minutes
Makes about 25

6 dried Chinese
  mushrooms
1 cup hot water
250 g beef mince
30 g pork fat, finely
  chopped
2 Chinese sausages,
  finely chopped
2 cloves garlic, chopped
3 spring onions,
  finely chopped
1 tablespoon sliced
  water chestnuts,
  drained and shredded
3 teaspoons sesame oil
2 teaspoons soy sauce
2 teaspoons Chinese
  wine or sherry
1 teaspoon cornflour

1. Soak the mushrooms in hot water for 10 minutes, drain and chop finely, discarding the hard stems.
2. Place the mince on a chopping board and finely chop with a large knife or cleaver. Place in a bowl with the pork fat, sausage, garlic, spring onions and water chestnuts.
3. Combine the sesame oil, soy sauce, wine and cornflour and mix to a smooth paste. Stir the paste into the beef mixture and mix thoroughly, kneading the ingredients together with your fingertips. Roll the mixture into small balls.
4. Line the base of a bamboo or metal steamer with a circle of baking paper. Arrange the Beef Balls in the base, spacing them well apart. (The Beef Balls may need to be cooked in batches.) Cover the steamer and cook over a pan of simmering water for about 10 minutes or until firm to touch and cooked through. Serve immediately with chilli sauce or sesame oil.

Note: Beef Balls can also be fried. Heat 2 cups oil in a wok or pan. Cook 4–5 Beef Balls at a time, over medium heat, turning occasionally, for 5–6 minutes or until dark golden brown. Remove with a slotted spoon and drain on paper towels. Beef Balls can be coated in cornflour before frying for a very crisp bubbly coating.

Note: The more finely chopped the mince, the finer and firmer the texture of the meatball will be.

Grilled Mushrooms with Sesame Seeds

Preparation time:
15 minutes
Total cooking time:
10 minutes
Serves 4–6

1 tablespoon sesame
  seeds
400 g medium flat
  mushrooms or
  shiitake mushrooms
2 tablespoons
  teriyaki sauce
2 tablespoons mirin or
  sweet sherry
1 tablespoon sugar
1 tablespoon finely
  chopped chives
1 teaspoon sesame oil
10 chives, cut into
  2 cm lengths

1. Preheat the oven to moderate 180°C. Line a baking tray with foil. Sprinkle the sesame seeds over the prepared tray and cook for 10 minutes or until golden.
2. Wipe the mushrooms with a damp cloth and remove the stalks. Put the mushrooms in a shallow dish. Combine the teriyaki sauce, mirin, sugar, chives and sesame oil. Pour over the mushrooms and allow to stand for 5 minutes.

❖ YUM CHA AND ASIAN TREATS ❖

Grilled Mushrooms with Sesame Seeds (top) and Beef Balls with Spicy Sausage

3. Place the mushrooms on a baking tray, brush with half the marinade and grill under a preheated hot grill for 5 minutes. Turn the mushrooms over, brush with the remaining marinade and grill for another 5 minutes or until browned. Garnish the mushrooms with the roasted sesame seeds and chopped chives to serve.

❖ YUM CHA AND ASIAN TREATS ❖

Tempura

The Japanese love of simplicity and freshness of ingredients is embodied in Tempura—morsels of fish or vegetable encased in a whisper of batter and fried to a light crisp finish.

Prawn Tempura
Preparation time:
  20 minutes
Total cooking time:
  15 minutes
Serves 4

8 raw king prawns
plain flour
oil, for deep frying
wasabi (see Glossary)

Batter
1 cup iced water
1 egg yolk
1 cup plain flour, sifted

Dipping Sauce
1/4 cup soy sauce
2 tablespoons
  lemon juice
2 tablespoons mirin
  (sweet Japanese wine)
1 tablespoon sake
  (Japanese rice wine)

1. Shell the prawns, leaving the tails intact. Remove the veins. Score the underside of the prawns with a sharp knife to prevent them curling. Press the prawns slightly to straighten them.
2. To make batter: Whisk together the water and egg yolk. Sprinkle flour over the top and stir in lightly with a fork or chopstick until just combined. (The mixture will be lumpy.)

3. Dust the prawns in flour, shaking off any excess. Dip in the batter (pushing any lumps to one side) and allow the excess to drain away. Deep-fry in hot oil until golden and crisp. Drain well on paper towels.
4. To make dipping sauce: Combine the soy sauce, lemon juice, mirin and sake in a bowl. Serve with dipping sauce and wasabi.

❖ TEMPURA ❖

Potato, Pumpkin and Onion Tempura
Cut potato and pumpkin into thin slices. Halve and slice the onions into rings. Dust in flour, shaking off the excess. Dip in Tempura batter, allowing the excess to drain off. Deep-fry a few at a time in hot oil until crisp and tender, turning during cooking. Drain on paper towels.

Vegetable Bundles
Cut carrots, beans, zucchini and spring onions into strips about 5 cm long. Arrange in bundles of 5 to 6 pieces on a plate. Sprinkle flour lightly over the prepared bundles.

Grasp the bundles with tongs or chopsticks. Shake off excess flour. Dip in Tempura batter. Carefully dip each bundle into hot oil. Fry, turning, until golden. Drain on paper towels.

Seafood Tempura
Cut boneless fish fillets into strips or small pieces. Cut calamari into rings or thin strips. Dust pieces in flour, shaking off excess. Dip fish and calamari in Tempura batter, allowing excess to drain off. Deep-fry a few pieces at a time until crisp, golden and cooked through (about 2 minutes for fish and 1 minute for calamari).

Hints and Tips
- The best Tempura is made using a thin crisping batter.
- Make the batter just before using as it becomes gluey if left for too long.
- Overstirring the batter will cause it to become too thick to use. *The batter will be lumpy.* An occasional stir will prevent the batter separating.
- Tempura should never be greasy— this is accomplished by keeping the oil at a high even temperature so it seals the outside.
- Test the heat of the oil by dropping in a small amount of batter. If it sizzles immediately, the oil is hot enough to use.

From left: Prawn; Potato, Pumpkin and Onion; Vegetable Bundles; Seafood Tempura

Five-spice Fish Balls

Preparation time:
  20 minutes + 30
  minutes refrigeration
Total cooking time:
  20 minutes
Makes about 20

200 g boneless fish
100 g raw prawn meat,
2 spring onions, finely
  chopped
2 teaspoons sesame oil
1/4 teaspoon five-spice
  powder
salt and pepper, to taste
oil, for shallow frying

1. Process the fish and prawn meat in a food processor until finely minced. Transfer to a bowl; add the spring onions, sesame oil, five-spice, salt and pepper.
2. Work together with your fingertips until thoroughly mixed. Chill for 30 minutes.
3. Form the mixture into small balls. Heat 1–2 cm oil in a wok or frying pan. Fry the balls in batches over medium heat, until golden brown. Drain on paper towels. Good with combined chilli sauce and sesame oil.

Notes: The balls may be rolled lightly in cornflour before frying to give a very crisp bubbly coating. If you prefer, chop the fish and prawns very finely with a cleaver—this gives a light texture.

Vietnamese Pancakes in Lettuce Parcels

Preparation time:
  20 minutes +
  45 minutes standing
Total cooking time:
  about 30 minutes
Serves 10

1 cup rice flour
2 teaspoons cornflour
1/2 teaspoon curry
  powder
1/2 teaspoon turmeric
1 cup coconut milk
1/2 cup water
1/4 cup coconut cream
2 teaspoons oil
150 g pork ribs, boned
  and thinly sliced
150 g raw
  prawn meat
4 spring onions,
  chopped
150 g bean sprouts
10 large lettuce leaves
1 cup fresh mint leaves

Dipping Sauce
2 tablespoons fish
  sauce
2 tablespoons lime juice
1–2 teaspoons chopped
  fresh chilli
1/2 teaspoon sugar

1. Place the flours, curry powder, turmeric, coconut milk, water and coconut cream in a food processor. Process for 30 seconds or until smooth. Cover and set aside for 45 minutes for the batter to thicken.
2. Heat 1 teaspoon oil in a heavy-based frying pan; add several pieces of pork and cook over medium-high heat for 1–2 minutes or until browned. Repeat with remainder; set aside.
3. Stir the batter well. Heat the remaining oil and add 2 tablespoons batter to pan, swirling to form a small round pancake. Cook for 30 seconds or until pancake begins to crisp on the underside. Pile 2 pieces pork, 1 tablespoon prawn meat, 1 tablespoon spring onions and 1 tablespoon bean sprouts in the centre of the pancake. Cover the pan and cook for 1–2 minutes, or until the prawns become pink and the vegetables have softened. (The base of the pancake will be very crisp, the top side will be soft and firm.) Place the pancakes on a platter. Repeat with the remaining ingredients.
4. Place each cooked pancake inside a lettuce leaf and top with

❖ YUM CHA AND ASIAN TREATS ❖

Vietnamese Pancakes in Lettuce Parcels (top) and Five-spice Fish Balls

2 mint leaves. Fold up the lettuce to form a parcel. Serve with dipping sauce.
5. To make dipping sauce: Combine the fish sauce, lime juice, chilli and sugar in a bowl and whisk until well blended.

Note: The pancake batter can be made up to 1 day in advance, adding 2 tablespoons of water if it thickens too much on standing. The pancakes can be made larger and cut into quarters or folded and cut if desired.

37

❖ YUM CHA AND ASIAN TREATS ❖

1 Gradually add the egg mixture, stirring to form a smooth batter.

2 Use a large sharp knife to cut away the drumstick from the duck.

Peking Duck Pancakes

Preparation time: 30 minutes
Total cooking time: 20 minutes
Makes about 15 pancakes

3/4 *cup plain flour*
1/3 *cup cornflour*
2 *eggs*
3/4 *cup water*
1/4 *cup milk*
2 *teaspoons caster sugar*
1 *tablespoon oil*
1/2 *large roasted Peking duck*
1/4 *cup hoi sin sauce*
1 *tablespoon Shaosing (Chinese) wine*
6 *spring onions, cut into 4 cm pieces and finely sliced lengthways*

1. Combine the flour and cornflour in a large bowl. Whisk together the eggs, water, milk and sugar in a separate bowl. Make a well in the centre of the flour and gradually add the egg mixture, stirring continuously with a wooden spoon to form a smooth batter.
2. Heat the oil in a frying pan and add 2 tablespoons of batter. Swirl the pan gently to form a round pancake. Cook over medium heat for 2 minutes or until crisp and golden underneath. Turn over and cook the other side for 10 seconds only. Transfer to a plate and place in a low oven to keep warm. Repeat with the remaining batter.
3. Using a Chinese cleaver or large sharp knife, remove the duck drumstick. Chop along the length of the remaining duck to make 2 cm long pieces, discarding the bone when finished. Remove the skin and bone from the drumstick and chop the flesh into even, thin slices.
4. Place heaped tablespoons of meat and skin on each pancake; top with the combined hoi sin sauce and wine, then sprinkle with shredded spring onions. Roll up and serve immediately.

> **HINT**
> Peking ducks are available from Chinese butchers. Some supermarkets have sections where you can buy roasted ducks, or use Chinese barbecue pork instead.

Peking Duck Pancakes

3 Cut the flesh of the duck into thin slices with a sharp knife.

4 Assemble the pancakes with the duck slices, spring onions and sauces.

Singara

*Preparation time:
45 minutes + 30
  minutes standing
Total cooking time:
20–25 minutes
Makes about 50*

1 teaspoon cumin seeds
1/2 teaspoon black
  mustard seeds
1/2 teaspoon
  fenugreek seeds
1/4 teaspoon
  fennel seeds
1/2 teaspoon chilli
  powder
1 tablespoon oil
2 cloves garlic, chopped
1 small onion, chopped
2 medium potatoes,
  (about 350 g) peeled,
  finely chopped
1/4 cup water
1 tablespoon
  lemon juice
salt and pepper, to taste
25 spring roll wrappers
oil, for deep-frying

1. Combine the cumin, mustard, fenugreek and fennel seeds in a spice mill or mortar and pestle. Mill or pound until roughly crushed then add the chilli powder. Heat the oil in a heavy-based pan; add the garlic and spices and cook for 2 minutes over low heat, stirring continuously. Add the chopped onion and potato and cook for 2 minutes, stirring constantly. Add the water, cover the pan and cook for 8 minutes, or until the potatoes have softened. Add the lemon juice and season with salt and pepper. Set the mixture aside for 30 minutes to cool.
2. Keeping the remainder covered and working with one wrapper at a time, cut each spring roll wrapper in half and moisten the edges with water. Place 2 teaspoons of filling at one end, leaving a small border. Fold the end of the wrapper over to form a triangle and keep folding to form a triangular parcel. Press the edges to seal and place on a baking tray. Repeat with the remaining filling and wrappers.
3. Heat 4–5 cm oil in a deep pan, add the parcels, in batches, and cook for 2–3 minutes or until golden brown. Drain on paper towels. Serve with a cooling mixture of finely chopped cucumber and plain yoghurt, if desired.

*Tandoori Chicken Pieces with Minted Yoghurt
(top) and Singara with yoghurt and cucumber*

Tandoori Chicken Pieces with Minted Yoghurt

*Preparation time:
25 minutes +
  overnight standing
Total cooking time:
45 minutes
Serves 4–6*

1.5 kg chicken pieces
juice of half a lemon
1/2 teaspoon salt
1/4 teaspoon
  cardamom seeds
2 teaspoons cumin seeds
1 teaspoon fennel seeds
3 teaspoons grated
  fresh ginger
3 cloves garlic, crushed
1 teaspoon
  chilli powder
200 g plain yoghurt
1 tablespoon
  butter, melted

Minted Yoghurt
200 g plain yoghurt
1 tablespoon chopped
  fresh mint
1 teaspoon sugar
1/4 teaspoon salt

1. Remove the skin from the chicken and make a few cuts in the flesh with a sharp knife. Rub the combined lemon juice and salt into the chicken. Heat a small frying pan; add the cardamom, cumin and fennel seeds and dry-fry over high heat

Yum Cha and Asian Treats

for 2 minutes or until fragrant. Transfer to a large bowl and add the ginger, garlic, chilli and yoghurt. Stir to combine; add the chicken pieces, cover and chill overnight.

2. Preheat the oven to 210°C and lightly brush an oven tray with oil. Put the chicken on the tray, brush with melted butter and cook for 45 minutes.

3. To make Minted Yoghurt: Put the yoghurt, mint, sugar and salt in a bowl, mix together and serve with the chicken pieces.

❖ YUM CHA AND ASIAN TREATS ❖

Dim Sum Scallops

Preparation time:
  10 minutes
Total cooking time:
  10 minutes
Serves 4–6

24 scallops on the shell
2 tablespoons
  teriyaki sauce
1 tablespoon soy sauce
1 tablespoon dry sherry
2 spring onions,
  finely chopped
2 teaspoons lemon or
  lime juice
2 teaspoons
  oyster sauce
1 teaspoon sesame oil
1 clove garlic, crushed
1/2 teaspoon grated
  fresh ginger

1. Preheat the oven to moderate 180°C.
2. Place the scallops, in shells, on an oven tray. Combine the teriyaki and soy sauces, sherry, spring onions, juice, oyster sauce, sesame oil, garlic and ginger in a bowl; stir to combine. Drizzle 1 tablespoonful over each scallop.
3. Bake the scallops for 5–10 minutes or until tender and white. (They can be cooked under a preheated hot grill for 5 minutes instead.)

Combination Dim Sims

Preparation time:
  1 hour + 1 hour
  refrigeration
Total cooking time:
  30 minutes
Makes about 30

6 dried Chinese
  mushrooms
1 cup hot water
200 g pork mince
30 g pork fat,
  finely chopped
100 g raw prawn meat
1 stick celery,
  finely chopped
2 spring onions,
  finely chopped
1 tablespoon sliced
  bamboo shoots,
  finely chopped
3 teaspoons cornflour
2 teaspoons soy sauce
1 teaspoon caster sugar
salt and pepper, to taste
30 won ton or egg
  noodle wrappers

1. Soak the mushrooms in hot water for 10 minutes, drain and chop finely, discarding the hard stems.
2. Put the mushrooms, pork mince, pork fat, prawn meat, celery, spring onions and bamboo shoots in a bowl. Combine the cornflour, soy sauce, sugar, salt and pepper in another bowl and blend to a smooth paste. Stir into the pork mixture. Cover and refrigerate for 1 hour.
3. Work with one wrapper at a time, keeping the rest covered. Place about 1 tablespoon of filling in the centre of each wrapper. Fold the corners in to the centre and press together to seal. Or, gather the wrapper in the centre like a pouch, gently press down the filling to firmly pack and tap on the bench to flatten the base. Put on a baking tray.
4. Line the base of a bamboo or metal steamer with a circle of baking paper. Arrange the dim sims on paper, spacing them well (they may need to be cooked in batches). Cover the steamer and cook over a pan of simmering water for 8 minutes or until wrappers are firm and filling cooked. Serve immediately with chilli or soy sauce.

Note: Dim Sims can also be fried. Coat them in cornflour for a crisp finish, then cook in 2 cups oil for 5–7 minutes. Drain on paper towels.

Combination Dim Sims (top) and Dim Sum Scallops

Sweet and Sour Spare Ribs

Preparation time:
  15 minutes
Total cooking time:
  1 hour + overnight standing
Serves 6–8

150 ml sweet and
  sour sauce
2 teaspoons
  chopped chilli
1 teaspoon cornflour
2 tablespoons
  dry sherry
2 tablespoons soy sauce
1/4 teaspoon five-spice
  powder
1/4 teaspoon grated
  ginger
6 cloves garlic, crushed
1.5 kg pork spare ribs,
  cut into small pieces
1 tablespoon
  chopped chives

1. Combine the sweet and sour sauce, chilli, cornflour, sherry, soy sauce, five-spice powder, ginger and garlic in a bowl; add the ribs and stir well, making sure all the ribs are well coated with the marinade.
2. Cover the bowl and refrigerate overnight.
3. Preheat the oven to moderate 180°C. Brush an oven tray with oil. Arrange the ribs on the tray and cook for 1 hour or until golden, turning every 20 minutes. Serve hot, garnished with chives.

Lemon and Lime Chicken Wings

Preparation time:
  20 minutes +
  overnight standing
Total cooking time:
  25 minutes
Makes 24

12 chicken wings
1 teaspoon grated
  lime zest
1 teaspoon grated
  lemon zest
juice of 1 lemon
juice of 1 lime
1 teaspoon oil
1/2 teaspoon sambal
  oelek
2 cloves garlic, crushed
2 tablespoons fresh
  coriander, chopped
salt, to taste

1. Cut the chicken wings in two (discard the tips if preferred).
2. Combine the zests, juices, oil, sambal oelek, garlic, coriander and salt in a shallow, non-metal dish. Add the chicken pieces and stir well to combine. Cover and refrigerate overnight.
3. Preheat the oven to moderately hot 210°C and brush an oven tray lightly with oil. Place the chicken pieces on the tray and cook for 20 minutes or until cooked through. Remove the chicken from the oven and place under a hot grill for 3–5 minutes or until crisp and golden, turning occasionally. Delicious, served with sweet chilli sauce.

Crispy Vegetables with Eastern Dressing

Preparation time:
  15 minutes
Total cooking time:
  5 minutes
Serves 6–8

200 g broccoli
200 g cauliflower
1 bunch fresh asparagus

Eastern Dressing
2 tablespoons oil
1 tablespoon sesame oil
2 tablespoons soy sauce
2 tablespoons lime juice
2 cloves garlic, crushed
1 teaspoon sugar
1/2 teaspoon grated
  fresh ginger
2 teaspoons fresh
  chopped coriander

1. Cut the broccoli and cauliflower into small florets. Trim the asparagus of any

❖ YUM CHA AND ASIAN TREATS ❖

From top: Crispy Vegetables, Sweet and Sour Spare Ribs and Chicken Wings

woody ends and cut in half. Plunge the vegetables into boiling water for 3 minutes so that they retain their crispness. Drain the vegetables and immerse in very cold water; this will help them retain their colour.

2. Drain the vegetables well, place in a serving bowl and serve with Eastern Dressing.

3. **To make Eastern Dressing:** Put the oil, sesame oil, soy sauce, lime juice, garlic, sugar, ginger and fresh coriander in a bowl and whisk until combined.

45

Satay Sticks

A Malaysian favourite... meat is marinated in spices, threaded onto skewers and served with a peanut sauce. Serves 4–6.

Malaysian Lamb Satays

Trim any fat or silver sinew from 500 g lamb fillets. Slice the meat across the grain into very thin strips. (This will be easier if the meat is chilled.) Combine 1 roughly chopped onion, 2 cloves garlic, 2 cm lemon grass (base section), 2 thick slices galangal, 1 teaspoon chopped fresh ginger, 1 teaspoon ground cumin, $1/2$ teaspoon ground fennel, 1 tablespoon ground coriander, 1 teaspoon turmeric, 1 tablespoon soft brown sugar and 1 tablespoon lemon juice in a food processor and process until smooth. Transfer to a shallow non-metal dish and add the lamb strips, stirring to coat well. Cover and refrigerate overnight. Thread the meat along bamboo skewers and cook under preheated grill for 3–4 minutes each side or until cooked. Brush with the remaining marinade while cooking. Serve with Satay Sauce.

Chilli Pork Satays

Trim the fat and sinew from 500 g pork fillet. Cut the pork into small cubes and place in a large bowl. Combine 2 tablespoons tomato sauce, 2 tablespoons hoi sin sauce, 2 tablespoons sweet chilli sauce, 2 cloves crushed garlic, $1/4$ cup lemon juice, 2 tablespoons honey and 2 teaspoons grated fresh ginger in a small jug or bowl. Pour over the pork and stir well to combine. Cover and refrigerate for several hours or overnight. Thread the pork cubes onto metal or bamboo skewers and cook on a lightly oiled preheated grill or barbecue flat-plate for 3–4 minutes each side or until cooked through and tender. Brush with the remaining marinade while cooking. Serve with Satay Sauce.

❖ Satay Sticks ❖

Satay Sauce
Combine 1 cup pineapple juice, 1 cup peanut butter, $1/2$ teaspoon garlic powder, $1/2$ teaspoon onion powder, 2 tablespoons sweet chilli sauce and $1/4$ cup soy sauce in pan. Stir over medium heat for 5 minutes until smooth. Add a little water if necessary.

Thai Beef Sticks
Trim 500 g fillet or rump steak of excess fat and sinew. Cut the beef into small cubes and place in a large bowl. Combine 2 teaspoons sesame oil, 1–2 cloves crushed garlic, 4 cm piece finely chopped lemon grass root, 2 tablespoons chopped fresh coriander roots and leaves, 1 tablespoon sweet chilli sauce, 1 tablespoon fish sauce, 1 tablespoon lime juice, 2 teaspoons soft brown sugar, 2 tablespoons each of fresh chopped mint and opal or purple basil and 1 tablespoon soy sauce in a small jug or bowl. Pour over the meat and stir to combine. Cover and refrigerate for several hours or overnight. Thread the meat onto skewers alternately with wedges of red onion. Cook on a lightly oiled preheated grill or barbecue flat-plate for 2–3 minutes each side or until tender. Brush with marinade while cooking.

Teriyaki Chicken
Cut 4 chicken breast or thigh fillets into small cubes and place in a medium bowl. Combine $1/3$ cup soy sauce, 1–2 tablespoons honey, 1–2 cloves crushed garlic, 2 teaspoons grated fresh ginger and 1 tablespoon sherry in a jug or small bowl. Pour over the chicken and stir well to combine. Cover and refrigerate for several hours or overnight. Thread 2 cubes of chicken alternately with 3 cm pieces of spring onion onto wooden cocktail skewers. Cook the skewers on a lightly oiled preheated grill or barbecue flat-plate for 2–3 minutes each side or until the chicken is tender and cooked through. Brush with marinade while cooking and serve with chilli sauce or yoghurt.

From left: Lamb, Pork, Thai Beef and Teriyaki Chicken skewers.

Spicy Prawn, Crab and Coriander Balls

Preparation time:
  25 minutes +
  30 minutes chilling
Total cooking time:
  15 minutes
Makes about 25

250 g raw prawn meat
225 g can crab meat, well-drained
3 cm ginger, peeled and grated
1 tablespoon fresh green peppercorns, crushed
2 egg whites
1 tablespoon fish sauce
1/2 cup coriander leaves
1 teaspoon fresh chopped chilli
1/2 cup rice flour
oil, for deep frying
lime wedges, to serve

Dipping Sauce
2 tablespoons fish sauce
2 tablespoons white vinegar
2 tablespoons lime juice
1/2 teaspoon sugar
2 tablespoons chopped fresh coriander

1. Combine the prawn meat, crab, ginger, peppercorns, egg whites, fish sauce, coriander and chilli in a food processor and mix until well combined. Stir in the flour, cover and chill for 30 minutes.
2. Heat 3–4 cm oil in a heavy-based frying pan; add rounded teaspoons of the prawn mixture and cook over medium heat for 3 minutes or until browned all over. (The balls may need to be cooked in batches; do not overcrowd the pan.) Drain on paper towels and serve with dipping sauce.
3. To make Dipping Sauce: Combine the fish sauce, vinegar, lime juice, sugar and coriander and whisk until well blended.

Note: The prawn mixture can be made a day in advance and refrigerated. Let it come back to room temperature for frying.

Lamb Pancakes

Preparation time:
  25 minutes +
  15 minutes standing
Total cooking time:
  30 minutes
Makes about 12

200 g lamb fillets
2 tablespoons soy sauce
1 tablespoon Shaosing (Chinese) wine
1 tablespoon finely shredded ginger
3 cloves garlic, chopped
1/3 cup cornflour
3/4 cup plain flour
2 eggs
3/4 cup water
1/4 cup milk
2 teaspoons caster sugar
2 tablespoons oil
2 tablespoons hoi sin sauce
3 spring onions, finely chopped

1. Trim the lamb of any sinew, chop into medium lengths and slice very thinly. Combine the lamb, soy sauce, wine, ginger and garlic in a bowl. Mix well and allow to stand for 15 minutes.
2. Combine the cornflour and plain flour and make a well in the centre. Add the combined eggs, water, milk and sugar and stir with a wooden spoon into a smooth batter.
3. Heat 1 tablespoon oil in a pan; add 2 tablespoons of the batter and swirl the pan gently to make a round pancake. Cook over medium heat for 2 minutes or until crisp and golden underneath. Turn over and cook the other side for about 10 seconds. Keep warm while cooking the remaining batter.
4. Heat the remaining oil in a pan, add the

❖ YUM CHA AND ASIAN TREATS ❖

Lamb Pancakes (top) and Spicy Prawn, Crab and Coriander Balls

lamb in batches and cook over high heat for 30–60 seconds or until browned. Add the hoi sin sauce to the pan; add all the cooked lamb, stir and remove from the heat. Place 1 tablespoon lamb mixture on each pancake, sprinkle with spring onion and serve.

Note: You will find that the lamb fillet is easier to finely slice for this dish if you put it in the freezer for 30 minutes beforehand.

❖ YUM CHA AND ASIAN TREATS ❖

Quail Eggs with Coriander and Mint Mayonnaise

Preparation time:
  20 minutes
Total cooking time:
  5 minutes
Serves 12

24 quail eggs
1 tablespoon fresh
  coriander
1 tablespoon fresh mint
1/2 cup mayonnaise
1/2 cup plain yoghurt
1 teaspoon curry
  powder
1/2 teaspoon sugar
salad leaves,
  for serving

1. Place the eggs in a pan of cool water and bring to the boil. Boil gently for 5 minutes then drain and immerse in cold water. (This will prevent the yolks discolouring.)
2. Finely chop the coriander and mint. Combine with the mayonnaise, yoghurt, curry powder and sugar in a bowl. Gently crack the eggs and peel off the shells.
3. Cut the eggs in half lengthways, arrange on the letttuce leaves and top with mayonnaise.

Prawn Gow Gees (top) and
Quail Eggs with Coriander and Mint Mayonnnaise

Prawn Gow Gees

Preparation time:
  30 minutes
Total cooking time:
  30 minutes
Makes about 30

250 g raw prawn meat,
  roughly chopped
4 spring onions,
  finely sliced
1 tablespoon
  grated ginger
2 tablespoons sliced
  water chestnuts,
  drained and chopped
3 teaspoons cornflour
2 teaspoons sesame oil
1 teaspoon soy sauce
1/2 teaspoon
  caster sugar
salt and pepper, to taste
30 gow gee
  dough rounds
sesame oil, extra,
  for glazing

1. Mix the prawn meat, spring onions, ginger and water chestnuts in a bowl. Put the cornflour, sesame oil, soy sauce, sugar, salt and pepper in another bowl; blend to a smooth paste, then stir into the prawn mixture.
2. Work with one dough round at a time and keep the rest covered. Hold a dough circle in the palm of your hand (this will keep the pastry warm) and put a rounded teaspoon of filling in the centre. Bring up two sides to meet and press the edges to seal. Press the gow gee firmly down on the bench to make a flat base and twist both sides down to form a crescent. Brush very lightly with sesame oil. Place on an oiled baking tray.
3. Line the base of a bamboo or metal steamer with a circle of baking paper. Arrange the gow gees on the paper, spacing them well apart. (They may need to be cooked in batches.) Cover the steamer and cook over a pan of simmering water for about 8 minutes or until the dough is slightly puffy and translucent. Serve immediately with sesame oil mixed with soy sauce, if desired.

Note: Steam gow gees within 1 hour of making—if the pastry becomes wet it is impossible to use. Freeze in single layers for up to 3 months. Do not defrost before cooking, but allow about 2 minutes extra cooking time.

Five-spice Chicken

Preparation time:
  20 minutes
Total cooking time:
  45 minutes +
  overnight standing
Makes 16

3 spring onions
4 cloves garlic
1 tablespoon sugar
1 tablespoon five-spice powder
2 tablespoons fish sauce
2 tablespoons soy sauce
2 tablespoons sweet chilli sauce
salt, to taste
16 chicken pieces
lime wedges, for serving

1. Finely chop the spring onions and garlic. Put in a bowl with the sugar, five-spice powder, fish sauce, soy sauce, sweet chilli sauce and salt and stir to combine.
2. Arrange the chicken pieces in a shallow, non-metal dish and spoon over the marinade. Turn the chicken to coat it thoroughly. Cover the chicken and refrigerate overnight.
3. Preheat the oven to 210°C and brush a baking tray with oil. Arrange the chicken pieces on the prepared tray and cook for 45 minutes, or until crispy. Serve warm with the lime wedges.

Char Sui Crisp

Preparation time:
  40 minutes
Total cooking time:
  20 minutes
Makes about 15

3 dried Chinese mushrooms
1/2 cup hot water
2 teaspoons oil
2 cloves garlic, chopped
3 spring onions, chopped
1 medium carrot, peeled and finely chopped
150 g char sui (Chinese roast pork), shredded
2 teaspoons oyster sauce
1/2 cup plain flour
1/4 teaspoon caster sugar
salt and pepper, to taste
1 tablespoon oil, extra
2 tablespoons Chinese wine or sherry
2 tablespoons cold water
oil, for shallow frying

1. Soak the mushrooms in the hot water for 10 minutes, drain and chop finely, discarding the hard stems. Heat the oil in a frying pan; add the garlic and spring onions and cook for 1 minute, stirring constantly. Add the carrot and char sui and then cook for another 2 minutes, stirring continuously. Add the oyster sauce and mushrooms, cover and steam for 1 minute. Remove from the heat and allow the mixture to cool completely.
2. Sift the flour into a medium bowl and add the sugar, salt, pepper, oil, wine and water. Beat with a wooden spoon until smooth and then stir in the char sui mixture. Form into small balls.
3. Heat 1–2 cm oil in a pan; add the balls, in batches, and cook over medium heat for 2 minutes, or until golden brown, then drain on paper towels. Repeat with the remaining balls, adding more oil if necessary. Serve immediately. Particularly good with char-grilled sweet potato, as shown.

Char Sui Crisp (top) and Five-spice Chicken

❖ Yum Cha and Asian Treats ❖

Fried Onion Crepes

Preparation time:
30 minutes
Total cooking time:
15–20 minutes
Makes about 30

1 cup plain flour
1 egg, lightly beaten
1/2 teaspoon sesame oil
1–2 tablespoons water
2 spring onions, finely chopped
3 tablespoons oil
sesame oil, extra

1. To make the dough, place the flour into a large mixing bowl, make a well in the centre and add the beaten egg, sesame oil and one tablespoon of water. Mix with a flat-bladed knife until mixture starts to form a soft dough, add more water if the dough appears to be too dry, only add a little water at a time. Gather the dough into a ball and refrigerate for 20 minutes.
2. Knead the dough on a lightly floured surface until smooth and elastic. Roll the dough out to form a large rectangle about 2 mm thick.
3. Brush the surface lightly with sesame oil and then sprinkle with spring onions. Fold the sides of the crepe into the centre to just meet. Flatten lightly then, starting at the bottom of the crepe, roll it up. Turn on its side, then roll out the dough to a thickness of 2 mm.
4. Using a 4 cm round cutter cut out circles and place to one side.
5. Heat 1 tablespoon of the oil in a shallow non-stick pan and cook the crepes on both sides until they are slightly puffed up and golden. Repeat with the remaining crepes, adding extra oil as necessary. Serve immediately.

> **HINT**
> These are delicious served with a dipping sauce made from sweet chilli sauce, a dash of soy sauce and a little lime juice. Try making crepes with the addition of some chopped fresh chives, basil or coriander. Sprinkle over with the spring onions.

Fried Onion Crepes on a bed of salad leaves

1 Cut in the dough mixture with a knife until it just comes together.

2 Knead the dough on a lightly floured surface until it is smooth and elastic.

❖ YUM CHA AND ASIAN TREATS ❖

3 Fold the sides of the crepe into the centre over the spring onions.

4 Use a 4 cm round cutter to cut out circles from the crepe dough.

Sweet Potato Fritters

Preparation time:
25 minutes
Total cooking time:
10–15 minutes
Makes about 30

1 cup plain flour
3/4 cup rice flour
1/3 cup cornflour
2 eggs, beaten
1 cup cold water
1 teaspoon salt
1/4 teaspoon black pepper
2 cups peeled and grated sweet potato
1 small spring onion, finely chopped
2 cloves garlic, chopped
1/2 cup bean sprouts, roughly chopped
oil, for shallow frying
30 small peeled cooked prawns

Dipping Sauce
1/3 cup white vinegar
1/3 cup cold water
2 cloves garlic, finely crushed
1 teaspoon salt

1. Combine the flour, rice flour, cornflour, eggs, water, salt and pepper in a food processor. Process for 1 minute or until smooth. Pour the batter into a bowl. Add the sweet potato, spring onion, garlic and bean sprouts and mix well.
2. Heat 1–2 cm oil in a pan. Using 2 spoons, push about 1 tablespoon of the mixture into the oil. Place a prawn on each fritter as it cooks. Cook each fritter for 2 minutes or until golden brown. Remove from the pan and drain on paper towels. Repeat with the remaining mixture and prawns. Serve immediately with a dipping sauce.
3. **To make Dipping Sauce:** Combine the vinegar, water, garlic and salt in a bowl and whisk to combine.

Black Satin Chicken

Preparation time:
15 minutes
Total cooking time:
1 hour
Serves 10

3 dried Chinese mushrooms
1/2 cup hot water
1/2 cup dark soy sauce
1/4 cup soft brown sugar
2 tablespoons Shaosing (Chinese) wine
1 tablespoon soy sauce
1 teaspoon sesame oil
1/4 teaspoon ground star anise or 1 whole star anise
1.4 kg chicken
4 cm ginger, peeled and grated
1 teaspoon salt

1. Soak the mushrooms in the water; drain, reserving the liquid. Combine the dark soy sauce, sugar, wine, soy sauce, sesame oil, star anise and reserved liquid in a small pan and bring to the boil, stirring continuously.
2. Rub the inside of the chicken with ginger and salt. Place the chicken in a large pan. Cover with the soy marinade and mushrooms, turning the chicken over so that it is evenly coated. Cover and cook the chicken over a low heat, turning regularly, for 55 minutes or until the juices run clear when pierced with a skewer. Remove the chicken and allow to cool briefly. Boil the sauce over high heat until thick and syrupy. Discard mushrooms.
3. Using a Chinese cleaver or large sharp knife, cut down the backbone to divide the chicken in two. Lay, cut sides down, on a chopping board and remove the wings and drumsticks. Cut the body of the chicken into 2 cm pieces; cut the drumsticks and

❖ YUM CHA AND ASIAN TREATS ❖

Sweet Potato Fritters (top) and Black Satin Chicken

wings in two. Arrange the chicken pieces on a serving platter, brush lightly with syrupy sauce and serve.

Delicious with sliced spring onions. Alternatively you could serve the sauce separately for dipping.

Note: Dark soy sauce is thicker in consistency than standard soy and is available from Asian food stores.

❖ YUM CHA AND ASIAN TREATS ❖

Empanadas

Preparation time:
  30 minutes +
  30 minutes standing
Total cooking time:
  40 minutes
Makes 24

Filling
1 tablespoon oil
4 rashers bacon,
  chopped
1 large onion,
  finely chopped
3 cloves garlic, chopped
150 g pork and
  veal mince
150 g chicken mince
2 tablespoons
  tomato paste
1 teaspoon soft
  brown sugar
1 tablespoon water
2 hard-boiled eggs,
  chopped
4 gherkins, finely
  chopped, optional
1/2 cup coriander
  leaves, chopped
1 egg white, beaten
oil, for shallow frying

Pastry
2 1/4 cups plain flour
1/2 cup water
1 egg, beaten
1 teaspoon caster sugar
50 g butter, melted

1. Heat the oil in a pan; add the bacon, onion and garlic and fry over medium heat for 5 minutes, stirring regularly. Add the meat and chicken mince and cook for another 5 minutes or until browned, breaking up any lumps with a fork. Add the tomato paste, sugar and water and bring the mixture to the boil, stirring. Reduce the heat and simmer uncovered for 20 minutes. Add the eggs, gherkins (if using) and chopped coriander. Set the mixture aside for at least 30 minutes to cool.

2. To make pastry: Combine the flour, water, egg, sugar and butter in a food processor and process for 20–30 seconds or until mixture comes together. Transfer to a floured surface and knead lightly. Cover with plastic wrap and leave to stand for 10 minutes.

3. Roll out the pastry to a 30 x 20 cm rectangle. Brush with butter and tightly roll the pastry up into a sausage. Cut into 3 cm slices and cover with a clean tea towel to prevent the pastry drying out. Roll out one slice of dough to an 8 cm circle. Place 2 tablespoons of filling in the centre and lightly brush the edges with egg white. Bring one side over to meet the other. Press the edges to seal. Decorate the edge with a fork, if desired. Place the filled pastry on a baking tray and repeat with the remaining filling and dough.

4. Heat 1–2 cm oil in a large pan, add the pastries and cook, in batches, for 2–3 minutes each side over medium heat. Drain on paper towels and serve.

Hint
Empanadas are now favourites in the Philippines. They are delicious as a small snack. Roll the circles of pastry into 16 cm rounds (ensure you cut the pastry into 5–6 cm slices). Put double the amount of filling in the centre, fold the pastry over and seal the edge. When cooking, add a little extra oil to the pan and extend the cooking time.

Empanadas

Spicy Chinese Sausage Rolls

Preparation time:
30 minutes +
25 minutes standing
Total cooking time:
30 minutes
Makes about 12

Dough
1 cup self-raising flour
2 teaspoons baking powder
1/4 cup warm milk
2 teaspoons caster sugar
2 teaspoons lard

Filling
6 Chinese pork sausages
2 tablespoons plum sauce or hoi sin sauce
2 teaspoons soy sauce

1. Sift the flour and baking powder into a bowl. Make a well in the centre, add the milk, sugar and lard. Mix to a soft dough with a wooden spoon. Cover the dough with plastic wrap and allow to stand 20 minutes.
2. Cut the sausages in half, place in a bowl with the plum or hoi sin sauce and soy sauce and stir to coat. Cover with plastic wrap and leave for 25 minutes.
3. Dust the bench with flour (use self-raising), tip out the dough and knead lightly with floured hands until soft and smooth. Roll the dough into a thick sausage 30 cm long. Cut into 16 pieces and cover with a clean tea towel to prevent the dough drying out. Working with one piece of dough at a time, rub the dough between lightly floured hands to form a thin sausage about 10 cm long. Wrap a dough piece around a piece of sausage in a spiral leaving the ends exposed. Place on an oiled tray and repeat with the remaining dough and sausage.
4. Line the base of a bamboo or metal steamer with a circle of baking paper. Arrange the sausage rolls on the paper, spacing them well apart. (The rolls may need to be cooked in batches.) Cover the steamer and cook over a pan of simmering water 12–15 minutes or until the dough is puffy and firm to the touch. Repeat with the remaining rolls and serve immediately with extra plum or hoi sin sauce, if desired.

Note: Chinese sausage (lup chiang) is a spicy pork sausage available fresh or in airtight packets from Asian food stores. Lard is essential to this dough and is available from the refrigerated section of supermarkets or Asian food stores.

Indian Prawn Fritters

Preparation time:
25 minutes +
30 minutes standing
Total cooking time:
20 minutes
Makes 15

350 g uncooked prawns
1 medium onion, roughly chopped
2 cloves garlic, chopped
4 cm ginger, grated
1–2 tablespoons curry paste
2 tablespoons lemon juice
1/2 cup coriander leaves
1 teaspoon turmeric
1/2 teaspoon salt
1/4 teaspoon cracked black pepper
1/2 cup besan flour (chickpea flour)
oil, for shallow frying

1. Shell and devein the prawns. Combine the prawns, onion, garlic, ginger, curry paste, lemon juice, coriander, turmeric, salt and pepper in a food processor. Process for

❖ YUM CHA AND ASIAN TREATS ❖

Spicy Chinese Sausage Rolls (top) and Indian Prawn Fritters

20-30 seconds or until well combined. Cover and refrigerate for 30 minutes.
2. Roll tablespoonfuls of mixture into round patties and lightly coat in besan flour. Heat 1–2 cm oil in a pan and add the fritters, in batches. Cook over medium heat for 3 minutes or until golden brown. Drain on paper towels and serve. Serve with plain yoghurt and lemon wedges, if desired.

Note: The different varieties of curry paste—Madras, Vindaloo, Korma, Green Masala and so on—have different spices, flavours and degrees of heat. Use whichever you prefer.

Dipping Sauces

Yum Cha dishes are often served with a sauce. You will find many scattered through the book. Here are a few more.

Sweet and Sour Sauce
Put 1 cup pineapple juice, 1/4 cup each sherry and white wine vinegar, 2 tablespoons soft brown sugar and 2 teaspoons soy sauce in a small pan. Stir over medium heat until dissolved. Blend 1 tablespoon cornflour and 1 tablespoon water in a small bowl and stir to a smooth paste; add to the pan and stir until the mixture boils, thickens and clears. Serve warm.

Thai-style Sauce
Seed and finely chop half a Lebanese cucumber. Put in a small bowl with 2 finely chopped spring onions, 1 finely chopped red chilli (seeded) and 1 tablespoon finely chopped coriander. Heat 1/3 cup caster sugar, 3/4 cup white vinegar and 1/4 cup water in a small pan and stir until dissolved. Cool and serve.

Hot Chilli Sauce
Combine 2 teaspoons sambal oelek with 1/3 cup rice wine vinegar and 1 teaspoon sugar.

Ginger Soy Sauce
Combine 2 teaspoons freshly grated ginger with 1/2 cup soy sauce. Add 1 crushed clove of garlic or some sweet chilli sauce to taste if you like.

Plum Sauce
Drain the contents of a 425 g can of plums and reserve the juice. Remove all the stones from the fruit and purée the flesh in a food processor. Combine the juice, purée, 1/2 cup of soft brown sugar, 1/2 cup of malt vinegar, 1 teaspoon grated ginger and 2 crushed cloves of garlic in a small pan. Bring to the boil, reduce the heat and simmer for 30 minutes, stirring occasionally. Serve at room temperature.

Clockwise from top left: Sweet and Sour, Ginger Soy, Hot Chilli, Plum and Thai-style sauces

❖ DIPPING SAUCES ❖

Index

Beef Balls with Spicy Sausage, 32
Beef Sticks, Thai, 47
Black Bean Pork Ribs, Chilli and, 24
Black Satin Chicken, 56

Calamari, Chilli, 8
Carrot Balls, 12
Char Sui Crisp, 52
Chicken
  Black Satin, 56
  Five-spice, 52
  Dumplings, 23
  Honeyed Pieces, 8
  Lemon and Lime, 44
  Tandoori Pieces 40
  Teriyaki Skewers, 47
Chilli and Black Bean Pork Ribs, 24
Chilli Calamari, 8
Chilli Pork Satays, 46
Chilli Sauce, Hot, 62
Combination Dim Sims, 43
Coriander and Mint Mayonnaise, 51
Coriander Balls, Spicy Prawn, Crab and, 48
Coriander Toast, Prawn and, 8
Corn Pancakes, Thai, 12
Crab and Coriander Balls, Spicy Prawn, 48
Crab and Prawn spring roll filling, 15
Crabmeat Dumplings, 23
Crepes, Fried Onion, 54
Crisp-fried Duck, 27

Dim Sims, 43
Dim Sum Scallops, 43
Dipping Sauces, 62–3
Duck Pancakes, 39
Duck with Lemon Sauce, Crisp-fried, 27
Dumplings, 22–3

Empanadas, 59

Fish Balls, Five-spice, 36
Fish Cakes, Thai, 24
Fish Skewers, Spicy, 12
Five-spice Chicken, 52

Five-spice Fish Balls, 36
Fritters, Prawn, 60
Fritters, Vegetable, 31
Fritters, Sweet Potato, 56

Ginger Pockets, Scallop and, 11
Ginger Soy Sauce, 62
Gow Gees, Prawn, 51
Grilled Mushrooms with Sesame Seeds, 32

Honeyed Chicken, 8
Hot Chilli Sauce, 62

Lamb Pancakes, 48
Lamb Satays, 46
Lemon and Lime Chicken Wings, 44
Lemon Sauce, 27
Lettuce-wrapped Spring Rolls, Vietnamese, 6

Minted Yoghurt, 40
Mushrooms, Grilled, 32

Onion Crepes, Fried, 54
Onion Tempura, Potato, Pumpkin and, 35
Oysters, Deep-fried, 18

Pakoras, Vegetable, 20
Paper-wrapped Prawns, 20
Peking Duck Pancakes, 39
Plum Sauce, 62
Pork and Tofu Dumplings, 23
Pork Dumplings, 22
Pork Ribs, Chilli and Black Bean, 24
Pork Satays, Chilli, 46
Potato Fritters, Sweet, 56
Potato, Pumpkin and Onion Tempura, 35
Prawns
  Crab and Coriander Balls with, 48
  Cutlets, 24
  Dumplings, 23
  Gow Gees, 51
  Indian Fritters, 60

Pancake Rolls, 29
Paper-wrapped, 20
Spring Rolls, Crab and, 15
Stuffed, 17
Tempura, 34
Toast, Coriander, 8
Pumpkin and Onion Tempura, Potato, 35

Quail Eggs, 51

Rice Balls, Steamed, 11

Samosas, 18
Satay Sauce, 47
Satay Sticks, 46–7
Sausage Rolls, 60
Scallop and Ginger Pockets, 11
Scallops, Dim Sum, 43
Seafood Tempura, 35
Singara, 40
Skewers, Spicy Fish, 12
Spare Ribs, 44
Spicy Chinese Sausage Rolls, 60
Spring Rolls, 6, 14–15
Sweet and Sour Sauce, 62
Sweet and Sour Ribs, 44
Sweet Potato Fritters, 56

Tandoori Chicken, 40
Tempura, 34–5
Teriyaki Chicken, 47
Thai Beef Sticks, 47
Thai Corn Pancakes, 12
Thai spring roll filling, 15
Thai Fish Cakes, 24
Thai Puffs, 31
Thai-style Sauce, 62
Tofu Dumplings, Pork and, 23

Vegetable Bundles, 35
Vegetable Fritters, 31
Vegetable Pakoras, 20
Vegetables, Crispy, 44
Vegetarian spring rolls, 15
Vietnamese Spring Rolls, 6
Vietnamese Pancakes, 36

Won Ton, Stuffed Prawns in Crispy, 16